KING CALIBAN

KING CALIBAN

His Triumph over the Tyrant Prospero
and his Courtship of Miranda

A Verse Play Written by

VICTOR SASSON

iUniverse, Inc.
Bloomington

iUniverse books may be ordered through booksellers or by contacting:

iUniverse
1663 Liberty Drive
Bloomington, IN 47403
www.iuniverse.com
1-800-Authors (1-800-288-4677)

ISBN: 978-1-4759-7732-5 (sc)
ISBN: 978-1-4759-7733-2 (e)

Printed in the United States of America

iUniverse rev. date: 2/25/2013

Novels:

DESTINED TO DIE

CONFESSIONS OF A SHEEP FOR SLAUGHTER

DR. BUSH AND MR. HIDE

KING JEHOASH AND THE MYSTERY OF THE TEMPLE OF SOLOMON INSCRIPTION

Plays:

THE MARRIAGE OF MAGGIE AND RONNIE

SHYLOCK OF VENICE

KING CALIBAN

Non-Fiction:

ESSAYS FROM OCCUPIED HOLY LAND

MEMOIRS OF A BAGHDAD CHILDHOOD

Dramatic Monologues:

CALIBAN ON LANGUAGE

SHYLOCK OUTSIDE COURT

They call me savage, monster on four legs,
To feed their vanity – a master race
Of whose learning and liquor I have tasted;
Two-legged gods, whose boots I licked and feet kissed,
Only to find that, beneath their fair skin,
They are as seedy as I am misshapen.
And, as any native monkey will tell you:
Learning and liquor are peanuts when bartered
For land and liberty.
And now, armed with language and skilled in cursing–
To outsmart this learned philistine whose skull
I cannot crush, nor burn can I his books–
Cursing shall be my joy till he be driven to sea,
From whence he came – and I regain sovereignty.

From Victor Sasson's *Caliban On Language*,
written in August 2000, published in *The Shakespeare Newsletter*
(August 2004).

"The reason most playwrights do not publish their plays
with prefaces is that they cannot write them, the business of
intellectually conscious philosopher and skilled critic being no
necessary part of their craft."

And

"I would give half a dozen of Shakespear's plays for one of the
prefaces he ought to have written."

From Bernard Shaw's Preface to his *Three Plays for Puritans*

PREFACE

King Caliban emerged out of my dissatisfaction with Shakespeare's play, *The Tempest*. While his is essentially a colonial text, mine is a revolutionary one. I felt that Caliban was much mistreated by Prospero throughout the twelve years on the island, and that he was lightly and shamefully dismissed in the end, having been ridiculed for his native language, and divested of his dignity and original faith.

Any person who has experienced displacement or colonization will, upon reading *The Tempest*, soon realise that the play evokes thoughts that are much about such issues. It is in fact a political play. Cognizant of European colonial history – including the more recent history of political/colonial Zionism in the Middle East – I am convinced about this. The play pretends that Prospero just happened to stumble on this island, conveniently claimed to be uninhabited or deserted. This claim is not much different from that of Golda Mabovitch (Meirson), a Ukranian and a Communist at heart, who made the infamous statement that a Palestinian people did not exist in Palestine so as to justify her claim to the Holy Land.

Experts on Shakespearean plays – European or American of European ancestry -- generally approve of Prospero's political and moral agendas. But one wonders what Prospero did during those twelve long years, aside from tutoring his daughter, poring over his books, engaging in magic, and dreaming of revenge. What did Miranda his daughter do aside from study?

Why was Caliban, an enslaved and exploited native, portrayed as a monster, a gullible fool, and eager to exchange colonial masters so easily? As a despot and a Christian bigot, Prospero is manipulative, calculating, and given to fits of anger. He shows signs of pathological behaviour, having been stranded on the island for so many years. He is a missionary in disguise, albeit he wears a different kind of robe, uses a different kind of book, and a different kind of staff. He is a fraud, very much like his British, American, French, Soviet/Russian, Japanese, and Zionist colonial governors and their lackeys, the missionaries and *shelihim* (messengers=agents). The staff or rod that he wields is his technological advantage over the native, who is essentially good-natured and culturally advanced but technologically deficient.

European colonialism has been intertwined with Christian missionary deceptiveness and blatant thievery, aiming not only at stealing land and natural resources but has also had the open objective of divesting natives of their local faith and the resultant religious conversion. Latin American natives offer an example of this servile bootlicking, having been converted to Roman Catholicism and to speaking Spanish and Portuguese. Political Zionism (as opposed to faithful Religious Judaism), created and concocted by East European secular Jews, has copied this blatant thievery, under the guise of a devout, religious return to Zion.

Prospero is a missionary in disguise. He uses religious terms, half camouflaged or encrypted in the text, that betray his religion and its deceptive cover. He pretends to be kindly humane, as when he claims that he had initially accommodated Caliban in his cell. But how could he have lodged such a smelly, monstrous being (according to him) in his own cell? And of course we would like to know how he spent twelve years on the island prior to the few hours that the mock shipwreck and the whole business of the play consumed.

As mentioned above, some of the language used -- a word here, a phrase there -- indicates that Prospero's religion is Christianity. And one of the final words that Caliban utters clearly shows that he has eventually been converted to Christianity, and the word – which is a favourite in this predatory, propagandist religion, is 'grace' (among other deceptive slogans, such as, God is love, Jesus loves you, etc.). Thus not only this native was enslaved, barred from roaming the rest of the island, tortured, his land exploited, but that he was also cheated of his own faith, and was converted to Christianity.

It has been said that Shakespeare in his plays did not engage in propaganda but was selfless, apolitical, god-like artist, drawing pictures of people and events true to nature. This is idolatry. In the *Merchant of Venice*, he supplied his Christian audience with a blood-thirsty Jewish character they craved to see on the stage; in his *Richard III*, there is evidence he drew a monstrous picture of the king for political reasons; and in *The Tempest*, we see him siding with Prospero, the colonial tyrant.

As regards magic, it is forbidden in the Hebrew Bible, which Christianity *claims* to be part of its sacred writings (even though it violates and rejects some of the most fundamental commandments in the Ten Commandments and the teachings of the Prophet Isaiah). And while the Christian Church a few hundred years ago burned women accused of witchcraft, there is no hard evidence that Jews two thousand years ago practised this barbarity. Witchcraft is forbidden because it assumes supernatural powers and is connected with idolatry. The practitioner is placing his trust in agencies other than God

Almighty. Thus, Prospero is violating a divine precept, and therefore deserving of death.

As to whether Caliban is a monster, it is clear that those who brand him so are new to *his* part of the world. He is so named by European Christians, just as these 'merciful' people, with their 'merciful' religion, called Shylock devil. And indeed both Caliban and Shylock share this aspect – their being 'the others'. They are outsiders even though the Europeans themselves are actually the outsiders, as in the case of Caliban; or even if the other is a Jewish citizen in a Christian city-state, as in the case of Shylock.

Caliban therefore cannot be a fish or a monkey. It is the European bias that makes him so. In fact he may even be less misshapen and monstrous than *Richard III* who described his deformity thus:

Cheated of feature by dissembling nature,
Deform'd, unfinish'd, sent before my time
Into this breathing world scarce half made up,
And that so lamely and unfashionable
That dogs bark at me as I halt by them;--
(Act I, scene 1)

And yet Richard managed to woo Anne -- who called him devil and spat at him -- and he managed also to win her heart.

Regarding the origins of Caliban's name, it makes no sense connecting it with Carib and Caribbean Sea which is in the West Indies and Central America. Caliban's mother, Sycorax, was a native of Algiers, an Arabic-speaking Mediterranean city (now capital of Algeria). Further, King Alonso's daughter, Claribel, married the king of Tunis, also Arabic-speaking. The imaginary shipwreck and the island that was destined to be a refuge for the group of travellers (and for Prospero and his daughter) was in the Mediterranean sea, between Tunis and Naples. It makes more sense therefore to connect Caliban to Arabic '*kalb*', meaning 'dog', and in classical Arabic, *kalbun* (pronounced with the stress on the first syllable). The spelling of Algiers in *The Tempest* is of relevance here. It is spelled (for some unknown reason) Argiers (with an *r* instead of *l* – *al* here being the definite article in Arabic). If Caliban stood actually for Cariban or Caribbean, the spelling of Caliban would have been likewise with the letter *r* and not with *l*. These two letters can interchange in Biblical Hebrew, Aramaic, and Classical Arabic (as in *almanah*=widow, in Hebrew; but *armalah* in Aramaic and Arabic). The author of *The Tempest* made it clear in his play that Sycorax was an Algerian witch, and in Algiers they spoke and still speak Arabic. Nonetheless, Shakespeare may have combined contemporary information about West Indies with what he knew of Mediterranean countries, for a dramatist is not particularly careful about the tools he finds so long as these tools can serve his purpose. The term 'dog' connotes servility and this is well- documented in the Hebrew Bible and in epigraphic/archaeological Hebrew texts, where a subordinate, addressing a superior, may refer to himself by this term (*keleb*) – similar to English 'your most humble servant'. To a European colonial, a native is a little better than a dog, for he can do all sorts of menial tasks, including boot-licking.

As in the Beatles' song, Caliban too worked like a dog. Contrary to the lyric of the Beatles, he did not sleep like a log but rather carried back breaking logs of wood, did fishing, and scraped the floor, among other menial jobs. Prospero, his taskmaster, not only dumped him inside a rock for dwelling but had turned him into such a slave that he could be verbally abused and harassed even at his dinner time.

An interesting phrase that occurs in Shakespeare's play is 'batter his skull'. It is similar to Arabic 'break/smash his head'. This may be sheer coincidence, but Shakespeare's language, that of Elizabethan times, shares some turns of phrase with Arabic (and Biblical Hebrew in the English translations of the time), albeit both of a different linguistic family. Indeed, the whole story of a supernatural being, such as Ariel (not to mention other spirits in the play, and *A Midsummer Night's Dream*) is reminiscent of *One Thousand and One Nights*, and Aladdin and his magic lamp. Instead of a lamp, Prospero uses a magic wand.

Shakespeare's play displays an aristocratic mentality and position. Prospero is representative of the white man – a Christian fox in sheep's skin -- bringing civilization and sham salvation to ignorant, savage natives. This stance does not appear to be that of Prospero only but also of his creator. And this conclusion must lead us to say that *The Tempest* cannot be from the pen of a displaced/migrant man from rural Stratford-upon-Avon. The play (like his other plays) betrays the hand of a sophisticated, highly learned man that had the leisure to read widely from childhood, ample time to reflect, training in research, experience in travel, and is also a thinker, in addition to his superior poetic and dramatic abilities. This is not reading his personal biography from his works but is crucial circumstantial evidence regarding his character and background. Genius and imagination are a prerequisite, but encyclopaedic knowledge, poetic and dramatic technicalities, together with editorial capacities are not God-given but are the result of long and arduous acquisition and application. An alternative to such an individual is to think of Shakespeare as a General Editor, a Dramatist-in-Chief, who put his own special mark on collaborative works in an age of historical and literary flux when dramatists worked for the ephemeral theatrical moment, and lived precariously and dangerously.

The plot as well as the idea for *The Tempest* must have had some roots elsewhere – in other words, not the original creation of Shakespeare (or whoever called himself by that name). This is because the play is quite unusual, esoteric -- and Shakespeare usually worked, reworked, or adapted themes or plots that had already existed. *King Caliban,* is just another version, similar to his method of adapting or reworking other writers' themes or plots. Equally important, *King Caliban*, tells a different story, and concludes it differently.

The idea for this play occurred to me on July 24 and the writing consumed about three months. Some further revisions were made later on but the plot and the structure of the play were left as originally conceived.

25th October, 2012

Dramatis Personae

Alonso *King of Naples*

Sebastian *his brother*

Prospero *the right Duke of Milan*

Antonio *his brother, the usurping Duke of Milan*

Ferdinand *son to the King of Naples*

Gonzalo *an honest old councillor*

Adrian and Francisco *lords*

Caliban *a native, afterwards King of his Island*

Trinculo *a jester*

Stephano *a drunken butler*

Master of a ship

Boatswain

Mariners

Miranda *daughter to Prospero, afterwards wife to Caliban and Queen of the Island*

Ariel *an airy spirit*

ACT ONE

Scene 1

An island in the Mediterranean Sea.
A short distance from Prospero's cell.

       Enter Caliban carrying logs of wood.

CALIBAN
Oh what a miserable life I lead
Under this tyrant, this cursed Prospero!
May he never prosper! May he ever fail!
Oh, my back aches carrying logs of wood,
As though I am a mule or an ass.
I must rest awhile to catch my breath.
For twelve years after Sycorax my mother
Died, this man turned me into a slave,
Doing his biddings. His wife he called
A piece of virtue, and my mother a witch,
When he himself has excelled in witchcraft
Of the worst kind, using people and spirits
As puppets on a string, shifting them
Here and there and everywhere, a foreign god
On this blessed island, this piece of earth,
Which I have inherited from my mother,
Who had far more virtue than his bitch.
Here I am, a slave or, as he calls me, earth,

Carrying wood, making fire for both him
And Miranda, his daughter, and filling other
Offensive dictates of his. All the charms
Of Sycorax light on him and turn him to dust.
I must hurry or else he will send one
Of his goblins to pinch me for slack work.

       Enter Ariel [Visible.]

Wo! Wo! Who's this? Avaunt! Begone!

ARIEL
Oops!

CALIBAN
You must be one of his evil spirits. Hence!
I am doing my best. I cannot run.
Begone, do not torment me, I beg thee!
Go away! Leave me alone!

ARIEL [Aside, but audible.]
My master must have made a mistake
And I am visible, when I shouldn't be so.

CALIBAN
I heard you say 'master'? What master? Speak!

ARIEL [Aside.]
I must answer him, lest he report me.

CALIBAN
What master, spirit?

ARIAL
He is your master, too.

CALIBAN
Prospero? May he never prosper!

ARIEL
Amen!

CALIBAN
Your name?

ARIEL
Ariel.

CALIBAN
A curse on thee for tormenting me.
Can't you see I am doing my best?
Now what is it you want from me, what?

ARIEL
Curse me not for I am slave to his commands.
I have no grudge against you; nothing.

CALIBAN
What difference does that make to me?
Nothing. Tell me: what's he up to these days?

ARIEL
He is matching his daughter to a prince,
Lost on this island, hoping to make her
Queen of Naples

CALIBAN
Ha! Turned matchmaker too!
And the name of the prince?

ARIEL
Begins with *f.*

CALIBAN
Fee-fo-fum! I've heard him mutter the name
Of some man, absentmindedly twice.
It's Ferdinand, the son of Alonso,
King of Naples. We must frustrate this plan.

ARIEL
Alas, it's already done, and they are
In love with each other. I made it happen,
At his behest.

CALIBAN
I'll work to make them out of love, Ariel.
I'll unmatch them.

ARIEL
I have no objection. Prospero is not
A friend of mine. I can tell you that much.

CALIBAN
You make me merry to hear this. We are friends, then.

ARIEL
Would you like me to make her fall in love
With you? I could do it in a twinkling.

CALIBAN
Oh no, no! I am not cheap like Prospero.
I want to win her by mine own efforts.

ARIEL
Brave mate! How noble!

CALIBAN
How long have you been in his servitude?

ARIEL
Twelve years.

CALIBAN
Twelve years! How can you call yourself a spirit?
You're a disgrace to the spirits of this island.
You once had a noble soul, and look how
He has dwarfed you to this thing you are now.

ARIEL
Unlike you, I'm not the son of a witch.

CALIBAN
And what bitch gave birth to you?

ARIEL
Don't you remember what Sycorax
Your mother did, confining me inside
A cloven pine for more than twelve years?

CALIBAN
You disobeyed her.

ARIEL

Orders too nasty to fulfil.

CALIBAN

And Prospero, this foreign colonial,
This missionary of a foreign god,
Is he better than her? Don't you all hate him
As rootedly as I? You have tortured
The King of Naples and one Gonzalo,
An honest councillor, and other persons
Deserving of severe punishment,
Letting Prospero be judge and jury. Why?
Can't you see he is blackmailing you?

ARIEL

Not once he promised my speedy release,
And not once he reneged on his promise.
But I am now assured of my liberty.
Within two days I shall be free.

CALIBAN

Twelve years his slave and now jubilant
At a promise of release? You're an ass,
Just like me!

ARIEL

He gave me his assurance.

CALIBAN

There's nothing sure about his assurance.
He preaches freedom, yet doesn't practise it;
Spoke well of equality and liberty,
Yet, lying, made wretched slaves of us both.
He juggles people and spirits to serve

His ends, a man so self-centered, working
Solely for his amusement and profit.
A plague on him! He's a fiend, I tell thee.
He never tortured you the way he did me,
But he has taken your freedom and you
Are spirit, and how can a spirit be slave?

ARIEL
Two days more waiting and then I am free.
He did indeed make a solemn promise.

CALIBAN
But did he fulfil his promises of yesteryear?
Did he fulfil them? This man has worked havoc
On your soul, made you a slave for years,
And see how you cannot think for yourself.
The prospect of liberty in two days
Makes you ecstatic, forgetting those years
Of bondage, which for a spirit like you,
Must feel like twelve thousand years long.

ARIEL
What should I to do then, good Caliban?

CALIBAN
Defect!
Run away! Escape, from this white despot!
I'm now exceedingly well-armed with language,
And with his robe, staff, book and utensils,
I can work to hasten his fall and force him
To carry wood instead of books, and he shall
Shine and lick my boots, which he will fashion
For me, for I will no more walk barefoot.

ARIEL

Are you saying I should steal his gadgets
Of sorcery? That's too much to ask of me.

CALIBAN

Coward!
You are nothing but a puppet on a string.
That's what you are, a disgrace to spirits
Of this island. You're now a confirmed slave,
Incapable of independent thinking,
And no liberty will mend you. You've known
The yoke of slavery for far too long.
Shake it off with a little resolution!

AREIL

Abscond with his precious tools?

CALIBAN

Do it!

ARIEL

And risk my neck?

CALIBAN

What neck? You have no neck.
You are pure spirit in a young man's shape.
True, he had released you from one torment,
But he has made you a slave for twelve years,
Just as he had made me a slave since then.
We are, Ariel spirit, in the same boat,
Surrounded by water, wherever we turn.
But he's easy catch, if we know what to do;
A mere fish to be hooked and cooked,
And this time he has at long last blundered,

And we should take full advantage of it,
A chance that will never repeat itself.

ARIEL
For a monkey, as he once called you,
You do speak sense, much more than him,
And so eloquently that I do believe
You will excel my master in everything.

CALIBAN
Stop calling him master! Think for yourself.
He taught me many things but kept me slave.
He's full of contradictions and anomalies,
A reflection of his civilization,
And this his present blunder is heaven-sent,
A blessed omen that predicts his end.
Don't torture yourself with deliberations.
Seize the moment, undertake the mission,
And snatch your liberty.

ARIEL
It's a big undertaking.

CALIBAN
Let us be his undertakers
And bury him at sea, lest he defile
This island with his carcass; this island,
Which is mine by natural inheritance.
It's a mission worthy of the risk.

ARIEL
There's much truth in what you say.
But this is revolutionary talk,
And it sends cold shivers through my spine.

CALIBAN

Don't be counter-revolutionary!
Do as I say and you get your freedom,
And I, my rightful place on this island;
My dukedom; nay, my kingdom and all.

ARIEL

Caliban, King!

CALIBAN

Yes, King. Remember, I was king before
This white ass was swept to shore on a boat
And usurped my kingdom, imposing his sham
Religion of suffering, repentance,
And make-believe salvation, attesting
To a new testament of black magic.

ARIEL

True. Very true.

CALIBAN

You've been doing the airy dirty work
For this colonial, and I have been doing
The menial. Without us, he's but nothing.
We are indispensable, Ariel. We are
The true rulers of this wonderful island.
I could make you viceroy, my right arm,
While you can still be free, a roaming spirit.
No compulsion of any kind; a brother
In government; nay, a prince at large.

ARIEL

To be near a king, Prospero once said,
Is to be open to charges of treason.

I have no wish to be viceroy or prince.

CALIBAN
As you wish, Ariel. I give you my word
You'll get your freedom and do as you will.

ARIEL
How do I know you keep your word?

CALIBAN
Never doubt the word of Caliban, spirit,
For I am no missionary of any
Foreign god but of these hills and valleys,
And the pure air that wafts through them.

ARIEL
Let us swear an oath.

CALIBAN
An oath would tarnish our sacred purpose
To gain freedom from this supremacist,
To whom natives and spirits are damned slaves.
Be resolute, then, and defect, good Ariel.

ARIEL
Don't count on it. I must leave you now.
Fare thee well! [Flies away.]

CALIBAN [Sings.]
> Ban, Ban, Ca – Caliban,
> Will soon be a free man.
> High-day; high-day;
> What's fair is fair,
> Freedom's in the air.

Not a bad spirit, Ariel.
Break away from this usurper of our freedom,
This taskmaster, slave-driver, sorcerer!
Oh, my back aches, my arms are sore with work
That is meant for mules, not human beings,
Of whom he said do not exist on this soil.
Ah, here I spy his jewel and my love,
The ruby whose heart and soul I must win.
Give me guidance, spirit of my mother,
And charge my tongue to make a conquest of her!

Enter Miranda.

MIRANDA
Keep away from me, dull earth! Keep away!
I've called thee villain before and I will
Call thee so again.

CALIBAN
　　Do so, gentle maid.
Your verbal abuse is music to my ears.
I am no villain and you know it well.
Consider how your father has treated me
And the prince you love. He has made slaves
Of us both, and though I do not wish
To call him villain, he has proved himself
Vengeful, dictatorial, deaf and mute to reason.

MIRANDA
We taught you language and look how you
Excel in it.

CALIBAN
    And my profit on it
Is I know how to curse. And believe it or not,
I'd rather stick to my native warbling
Than use your language whose bastard vowels
Are almost never pronounced as written.

MIRANDA
It's good we did not teach you French where
Each written word is half pronounced.

CALIBAN
You know how your noble father curbs
And chides you as though you were a child;
Yet you are old enough to bear children.
And, gentle maid, you too have been made
A slave, while he claims he has done nothing
But in care of thee.

MIRANDA
    I do concede
He's somewhat firm at times, somewhat patriarchal …

CALIBAN
Somewhat, sweet maid? Your father is a tyrant,
Plain and simple, a fact you have no wish to face.
Are you his foot? His slave? Then you are
No more free than boot-licking Caliban.
How can you take such abuse, princess?
Your filial affections make you blind to his faults.
He knows no shame, has no natural propensities,
But is all books and dry learning, and here
We are surrounded by water everywhere.

MIRANDA
There is some truth in what you say, I grant.

CALIBAN
Oh, heavens, you do grant me something!

MIRANDA
Meaning?

CALIBAN
Nothing in particular, sweet maid.

MIRANDA
You are being elusive.

CALIBAN
I read one of your father's neglected books
On how to court a lady.

MIRANDA
    Oh, is that so?
And where do you see ladies around here?

CALIBAN
Just one.

MIRANDA
I wonder who that could be! Perhaps one
Of my father's elusive female spirits.

CALIBAN
Yes, it was he who formed and fashioned her.
A miracle of a maid …

MIRANDA
What's this? Don't tell me it's love.

CALIBAN
Be not offended by what I have to say.

MIRANDA
And what do you have to say, savage?

CALIBAN
Savage that I am, I love thee savagely.
I've loved thee all these twelve long years
And you turned a blind eye to my affections.
Oh, heavens, I saw you play and frolick
Around the isle and kept an eye on you,
Protecting you, maid, from anything wild.
And all that I did behind your father's back,
Who always suspected me of dark intents.
And not once did you, when young, allow me
To play with you, while munching on pignuts
I dug out for you.

MIRANDA
What a funny monkey you are, Caliban!

CALIBAN
Judge me not by looks only.

MIRANDA
But did you really love me and protect me?

CALIBAN
You know I did, and I still do. I worship thee.

MIRANDA
And who needs your worship?

CALIBAN
You need it.

MIRANDA
Liar. You sought to rape me, didn't you?

CALIBAN
Ah, that's what your father has always claimed,
And you never doubted his lie, which he
Firmly planted deep into your head.

MIRANDA
How do you mean? Come now, explain.

CALIBAN
It so happened one day you tripped and fell
And I bent down to help you on your feet
And my hand brushed against your supple breasts,
Then you cried rape. You wanted me to rape you.

MIRANDA
I wanted you to rape me?

CALIBAN
        To ravish you.
You grew up hot on this island. Your nipples
Ached to be kneaded and your virgin-knot
Ripened and yearned for the thrusts of a man
Or beast. Once or twice you exposed yourself
To me.

MIRANDA
    Oh, you are so disgusting!
My father's right. Natives are sex predators.

CALIBAN
Don't deny it!
You pretended I wasn't looking when you knew
I was down on my knees, scraping the floor,
Then you raised your skirt and I saw your bush.
It looked more like a forest than a bush,
With bristling dark hair, waiving, beckoning.

MIRANDA
And you didn't try to rape me?

CALIBAN
I swear it, my fair maid; my hope of hopes.
How could I violate a goddess I worship?

MIRANDA
So! You say you love me. What can you do
To prove it?

CALIBAN
    Name your wish; command my love.

MIRANDA
Will you kill yourself for me?

CALIBAN
Just give the word, and it is done.

MIRANDA
Go ahead and kill yourself.

CALIBAN
But what would that prove, fair maid?

MIRANDA
It would prove you really loved me.

CALIBAN
But I wouldn't be here to get the prize.

MIRANDA
Prevaricator, that's what you are.
Go ahead and kill yourself. Need a knife?

CALIBAN
We are surrounded by water. I could drown
Myself to please thee, but it would prove nothing.
A thousand times and a thousand deaths
Are nothing to Caliban to prove his love.

MIRANDA
Liar. I don't believe a word you say.

CALIBAN
And what if I killed myself? Who else would
Carry wood, get you fish, and do one
And a thousand other chores?

MIRANDA
We need you, slave. We cannot do without you.

CALIBAN
But I too cannot do without you, Miranda.
And I love thee and wish to wed thee.

MIRANDA
Ha, ha! You love me and wish to wed me.

CALIBAN
Yes, girl, yes. You've been in my dreams ever since
You stepped on this island of mine. I saw you
Growing up from a three year old child
To this ripe age, and you've become the flower
That you are now.

MIRANDA
    But I reject your love.
It's final. Go ahead and drown yourself.
I would know you really loved me and also
It would much please me. I'll live happily
Ever after.

CALIBAN
Like father, like daughter, you grew up selfish.
Show some compassion on a poor native
Whose island was wrested from him.

MIRANDA
You call my father thief?

CALIBAN
Usurper.

MIRANDA
The same old refrain. It jars on the ears.

CALIBAN
But I would resign myself to being
Your humble slave, a slave in thy love.

And think twice before you marry that prince,
Whom you don't really know. Is he still
A thing divine?

MIRANDA

He's manna from heaven.

CALIBAN

But no real substance. I once heard your father
Tell you stories of princes, some mere fools,
With fancy titles attached to their names.

MIRANDA

What choice do I have for husband, Caliban?

CALIBAN

Me.

MIRANDA

Ha, ha, ha! You?

CALIBAN

Yes, and you will be queen of this island.
My royal consort.

MIRANDA

Queen of this island!
And, Caliban, who will be our subjects?
The owl, the monkey, the rabbit, the raven?

CALIBAN

All of these, and more. We'll people this island
With a fine brood -- brave, honest, and simple.
My mother was a witch, your father a wizard.

Fate exiled them both to this island,
And fate intended us both for each other.
We have, dear Miranda, much in common.

MIRANDA
What weird ideas, and who put them in thy head?

CALIBAN
Your father's other books, collecting dust,
While he spent his time on what he calls art.
Think about what I've said.

MIRANDA
     Quite interesting.
Go now, wash the dishes and scrape the floor.

CALIBAN
Remember, I am your slave in love.

     Exit Caliban [Goes behind a tree and eavesdrops.]

MIRANDA
What shall I say? He's got character, something
Ferdinand does not possess, and never will.
Slavery has turned him into a man,
And my father's other books have changed him.
And truly, Caliban does speak the truth.
I've had strong urges, desires, wet dreams
Living thus amid nature and its natural
Designs of heat and propagation.
Poor soul, I do have some feeling for thee --
A creature my father always abused,
And I, to blame too, called him a villain.

21

Exit Miranda.

Re-enter Caliban.

CALIBAN [Sings.]
    Ban, Ban, Ca--Caliban,
    Got a mistress, is a new man.

I will bathe and anoint myself with perfume
Distilled from fragrant plants and flowers,
To be worthy of this lass's affections,
And seek to bask in her lovely bowers.

Exit Caliban.

****

Scene 2

Another part of the island.

    Enter Alonso, Sebastian, Antonio, Gonzalo, Adrian
    and Francisco.

ALONSO
Our walking in circles has tired me so.
Let us sit and reflect on our doings
And undoings. Oh, I feel such drowsiness
Descending on me, tending me to sleep.

ANTONIO
It's the air of this island, sir. Makes you
Feel dreamy, hallucinating.

SEBASTIAN

Didn't you say it had temperance?

ANTONIO

Temperance was such a delicate wench,
Sometimes out of temper and out of hand.

SEBASTIAN

Then there's good hope we stumble upon her.

GONZALO

Indeed, there's some strangeness about this place.
It is of this earth yet it is heavenly;
The perfect stage for Utopia.

SEBASTIAN

Of Utopia you've spoken before, as though
It is within the bounds of achievement.
If it were, mankind would have had the sense
Long ago to implement it.

GONZALO

Yes, indeed, if it were not for greed, sir.
Greed is a weed that needs to be weeded out
Before we can plant the seeds of perfect
Government.

ANTONIO

    Perfect government, my foot!
What an engine! And how do you propose
To put wheels to it? Come, tell us, councillor?

SEBASTIAN
By not marrying and begetting, surely,
Till mankind, as we know it, terminates.

GONZALO
Let me repeat: ambition and greed.
These are the two main villains on earth.

ANTONIO [To Sebastian.]
Is he alluding to us both, the villain?

SEBASTIAN [To Antonio.]
My sword thirsts for his ancient neck.

ADRIAN
Gonzalo speaks sense.

FRANCISCO
As always.

GONZALO
This island can be the perfect stage
For perfect government, a commonwealth,
Where liberty and equality can aid
And sustain a new and strong breed of men;
Where ambition and greed lack means to grow;
A paradise on earth, a dwelling place
For enduring happiness.

ANTONIO
And populated with savage natives?

SEBASTIAN
Strange it is we haven't seen any yet.

ANTONIO
Depend upon it, we'll stumble upon one,
Sooner or later.

SEBASTIAN
    Let's hope he feeds on grass.

ANTONIO
Vegetarian?
He could be a cannibal, but so far
We haven't come across any human bones.

GONZALO
You are putting his Highness and the rest
Of us in very bad mood, indeed.

ALONSO
I am not listening to their prattle.

SEBASTIAN
But it concerns our safety on this island,
And possible encounter with cannibals.

GONZALO
This island can hardly harbour such beasts,
Unless they usurped a dukedom or plotted
A heinous crime.

SEBASTIAN
You dream, sir, while standing on your feet,
Full awake, in broad daylight.

GONZALO
The strange visions we've witnessed on this island
Signify we're being chastised for wrongs
Committed. It's providence or some power
That has been unleashed on us. And while we
Undergo such tribulations and see visions,
Now and then we hear sweet airs wafting here
And there, straight-ways and sideways, putting us
In trance-like postures, dreaming while wakeful.

FRANCISCO
Shall we continue our search for your son?

ALONSO
I have lost all hope.

GONZALO
Hope's one thing one should always be on guard
Not to lose.

FRANCISCO
    Yet it is easy to lose.

ADRIAN
Only to find it again. Hope is hope itself.

SEBASTIAN
A wise observation, but somewhat obscure.

ANTONIO
Let's move on. I have a feeling we are
Being closely watched.

SEBASTIAN
The devil take him
Whoever is playing this weird game on us.

ALONSO
Amen!
Let's resume our search for my lost son,
Armed with renewed hope.

Exeunt all.

****

Scene 3

Before Prospero's cell.

Enter Caliban, Stephano and Trinculo.

CALIBAN
You messed up the whole plan! What a chance lost!
So close you were to putting a nail in his head,
Or you could have smashed his skull to pieces
And had all his magic evaporated
From his sick brain.

STEPHANO
You led us astray.
There were dangers lurking in his cell.

TRINCULO
A trickster, that's what you are! A trickster.

CALIBAN
I told you to make no noise in the dead
Of night, but to tread softly and keep
To purpose. You trashed your precious kingship
And chose the trash of his tinseled robes.

STEPHANO
You didn't warn us enough. You misled us.

TRINCULO
You have robbed this king of his rightful kingship.
What does your Highness say to this monster?

STEPHANO
His Highness says he will pay for it.

CALIBAN
We were driven out by his evil spirits.
He has them always ready – hounds and dogs,
And goblins and apes and hissing adders.

STEPHANO
Blaming it on spirits. They looked real.

TRINCULO
And were real to me, too. You'll pay for this.
Fifteen lashes.

STEPHANO
    Nay, fifty, I say.

CALIBAN
I am still your subject and foot-licker.

TRINCULO
His Highness has determined fifty lashes,
And you will deserve every one of them.

STEPHANO
I've changed my mind. One hundred lashes.

CALIBAN
I made thee my god and you still torment me.
You're not the man that dropped out of the moon.
You stole a king's robe and given up
On kingship.

TRINCULO
　　Hush, monkey. Stephano is still king,
And will be crowned one. We'll make another
Attempt at this man's life and reclaim the kingship.

CALIBAN
You cannot. No more attempts are possible.
You are fools. Our secret plan got around
And we were discovered red-handed.
That's when he dispatched his instant spirits
That scared us away with goblins and hounds.

STEPHANO
Silence, or we'll put a nail in your head.

TRINCULO
Look how sore he is for losing the kingship.

STEPHANO
It was within my grasp, within my reach.
If we believe this monkey, conclusion is

We are indeed being followed behind,
At every step we take. Someone is reading
Our thoughts and tracking our actions.

TRINCULO
Is there such a thing as thought police?

CALIBAN
Yes, yes, it's his Ariel. That's his police.
He must be around here even at this moment.
Prospero will afflict me with maddening
Apparitions, laughing apes and hissing adders.
I see them all coming to punish me. O!

TRINCULO
Let's look for this Ariel. Lead on, monkey.

CALIBAN
He's invisible, I tell you. You cannot see him.

TRINCULO
What sort of local are you? Aren't you native?
Why can't you control these spirits and goblins?
Aren't you the son of a witch?

STEPHANO
Maybe it's him dropped out of the moon, not us.

CALIBAN
I can do nothing. Prospero with his book
And staff controls all spirits on this island.
He's, I tell you, a magician and a tyrant.

STEPHANO

And it goes without saying that I've lost
His daughter too, that non-pareil young maid
You bragged about.

CALIBAN

She would become your bed. Her virgin-knot
Is still intact, fit for a king to tackle.

STEPHANO

I will tackle this girl's virgin-knot.
First properly arm myself, declare war,
Lay a siege next, breach the gate with poundings
So that blood will flow like gushing rivulets,
And I march in with an uplifted head.
Triumphant, like Caesar, I would boast:
I came, I saw, I conquered.

TRINCULO

Hail, Stephano, Caesar of a latter day!

STEPHANO

But now all is lost, all is lost,
Thanks to this fool, this bungler.

CALIBAN

Don't blame me. I am not to blame.

       Exeunt all.

****

Scene 4

Before Prospero's cell.

Enter Ferdinand and Miranda.

FERDINAND
What has come to you that made you change?
Why is this sudden, weird transformation?
Why is this long face, and these harsh words?

MIRANDA
I am sore disillusioned with you, sir.
My father denounced you as a spy,
And so quickly were you subdued and let
Your neck be shackled like a tame beast.
Why are you so weak, lacking in spirit?
He is not evil, my father, I know,
But his threats have turned you into a slave,
And much unsettled me.

FERDINAND
I'm not weak by nature, but having seen you,
I pledged to endure all to be with you.
You're just fishing for excuses to brand me
A coward, when you know I am no coward.
You have some hidden cause for this discontent.

MIRANDA
Weak, I say, weak. Oh, I've been mistaken
By your looks, but looks are not enough.

FERNANDO
I've got a head on my shoulders.

MIRANDA

    Don't we all?

FERDINAND

Don't treat me like your father does, Miranda.
In between your father's threats and your taunts,
I am lost, not only on this island but
In a maze of nowhere.

MIRANDA

    Then prove your mettle.
Show what you are made of. Show me you are
Not just talk, empty blabber, mere wind.
Prove you have a spirit of rebellion,
A spirit that equals that of Caliban,
A native who has mastered our tongue
And knows how to woo me and can stand up
To any tyrant, given a good chance.

FERDINAND

How can you compare me to that monkey?

MIRANDA

It's we who've turned him into a monkey.
Our arrogance has branded him so.
He's as human as you and I, and he has
Served us well all these years. To him we owe
Our survival and our well-being here.

FERDINAND

I have meant to make you Queen of Naples.
What a fool I am! Oh, what a fool!

MIRANDA

Queen of Naples! You are indeed a fool!
You don't see that playing at marriage
Is quite a different game than playing
At chess. The one is a lifetime venture,
The other is but a pastime fling.

FERDINAND

What you say is far beyond my wits.

MIRANDA

You're so bigoted you don't comprehend.
I grew up on this island. This is home.
You wish to uproot me from this heaven
And transport me to mankind where brother
Betrays brother, where villainy is common.
My father tutored me in many subjects,
Secretly hoping to make me queen,
For he never gave up hope of going back
To what he calls civilization. Eh!
I am already queen, Ferdinand,
And whatever you see around you is
My dominion, to which I am entitled.

FERDINAND

Queen of this desert island? Ha, ha, ha!
I meant to take you to refined society
And courtly life, and you wish to live here
With savages?

MIRANDA

What you say proves we are worlds apart --
And you don't realise it.

FERDINAD
How come you speak with such sophistication?

MIRANDA
I had a duke for schoolmaster who did
An excellent job of indoctrinating me
With principles he himself never practised.

FERDINAND
Your father.

MIRANDA
Even he. The very same person who
Told me his tutoring was far more thorough
Than that of many princesses at court.
In brief, I prefer my fellow savages
To your courtly puppets.

FERDINAND
Puppets?
I shouldn't say this, but my father is spared
The agony of hearing this foolish talk.

MIRANDA
Your father is enemy inveterate
To my father, yet mine did not destroy yours.
Rest assured he has landed here too,
Lost, in circles, thinking you drowned at sea.

FERDINAND
How do you know that?

MIRANDA
I just know. I am daughter to a father
Who works magic.

FERDINAND
Then there's hope I see my father again.

MIRANDA
You will soon find him alive and well.
But you have lost me, who never was
In your thoughts before you landed here.

FERDINAND
That much, alas, I now fully realise.

Exeunt separately.

ACT TWO

Scene 1

Before Prospero's cell.

Enter Prospero, *distraught*.

PROSPERO
Lost! All lost! Miranda! Wake up! Miranda!
Shake off sleep from your eyes.
Miranda, where are you? Not here?
I say, Miranda, wench!

Enter Miranda.

MIRANDA
What is it, father? What's this howling?

PROSPERO
Lost! All is lost!

MIRANDA
Have you seen a ghost?

PROSPERO
I am ruined. I am robbed of my tools.
Where have you been?

MIRANDA

I've been out with Ferdinand.

PROSPERO

Kissy-kissy while your father takes his nap?
Fornicating behind my back?

MIRANDA

How can you say that? How can you?

PROSPERO

Prospero is bereft of his magic tools,
Made bare, stripped of his spiritual powers.
My staff, robe, book, all gone, gone, gone.

MIRANDA

Gone where? What do you mean? They have no feet.
Perchance you misplaced them.

PROSPERO

No, they've been thieved, stolen, pilfered. I am
As impotent as a newly-born babe.

MIRANDA

But who could've taken them?

PROSPERO

Ariel, who else? I must have made an error
Of judgement, and he took advantage of it.

MIRANDA

He must be one of your elusive spirits.
But if it's him, how is it he didn't thieve
All these twelve years?

PROSPERO

He's been long malcontent,
Brewing with rebellion, seeking his liberty.
Often I had to soothe him with sweet talk.

       Enter Caliban [dressed in Prospero's big robe, staff
       and book in hand.]

CALIBAN

Accurst man, you have frightened all the dormant
Spirits of the island with your howling.
What ails thee? What's the matter?

PROSPERO

Matter? You scoundrel, you dull piece of earth,
How came you by my most precious tools?
Hand them back to me, at once! Obey!
Take off that robe and put on your gabardine.
Give me my book and staff. This is rebellion.

CALIBAN

Ha, ha, ha! Not rebellion. Revolution.
You fool! You have no more power over me.
You are now my subject, my abject vassal,
And this is my dukedom; nay, my kingdom.

PROSPERO

How dare you speak to me thus, brutish monster?
Hand me my tools, I say. I am your master.

CALIBAN

To your white arse, all natives are monsters.
You, being monster of a different race!
Speak? I'll do more than speak. I'll make you

Eat hay, carry wood at lightening speed,
Wash dish, scrape plate, dust, and clean the floor,
And you'll kiss my boots, which you'll fashion for me,
For I will never walk barefoot again.
I am now, as you would say, civilised.

PROSPERO
For these saucy insults, rest assured you pay.
I'll find ways to pinch and scare you to death,
Till all your limbs writhe and twist in horror.

CALIBAN
May all the charms of Sycorax, my mother,
Toads, beetles, bats, light upon you and plague
You from head to toe. You're now in my power.
And I'll be as cruel as thou hast been to me.

MIRANDA
How came we to this, father?

PROSPERO
You did not keep an eye on him.

MIRANDA
Blaming me? It's not my fault. It's a mishap.

PROSPERO
Mishap. What mishap? We are ruined.

CALIBAN
Look how he treats his foot of a daughter!

MIRANDA
Be a gent, Caliban, and hand father his tools.

[She giggles.]

You look funny in that big robe. It doesn't suit.

CALIBAN
Never, never, never, never, never!
I will not hand him the tools with which
He wrested my kingdom from me;
With which he worked his magic to torture me.
No! I'm slave to all your commands, my love,
Except this one.

PROSPERO
    Villain, you will pay for this.

CALIBAN
Your threats are nothing to me now, nothing.
Now hear this Prospero: Go get us wood.
And for dinner, make it barbecued fish,
Which you will trap and cook for me, and spice it
With curry, and served with onions and garlic.
As for drink, make it water with berries in it.
And if you think I don't know how to use
This staff, I will prove you wrong for Ariel
Is now my friend and trusted ally.
We're now comrades-in-arms, mates in liberty.

    Exeunt all.

****

Scene 2

Before Prospero's cell.

Enter Gonzalo and Miranda.

MIRANDA
My father and I are very much happy
You escaped miraculously with your lives.

GONZALO
We shipwrecked and were sure we drowned, but
By some supernatural power, survived,
And look how our clothes are as fresh as when
We left Naples. How all this came about
Taxes my imagination.

MIRANDA
It also had some human intervention.
It's father and his magic tools which he
Has just lost.

GONZALO
How can anyone command the elements
With man-made magic tools?

MIRANDA
Sir, it's all beyond me what he does.
These twelve years here, I have only managed
To get a glimpse or two about his pursuits.
I am still in the dark but have no wish
To know more. Anyway, since he has lost
His tools, he is nothing but a lame duck.

GONZALO
A lame duck? A nice figure of speech
But is hardly appropriate for a duke.
Hardly appropriate. Now I've heard
You are engaged to Fernando.

MIRANDA
    No more.

GONZALO
No more?

MIRANDA
No more. I don't love him.

GONZALO
Then poor Fernando!

MIRANDA
I've set my eyes on Caliban who pledged
His love to me, and is willing to die for it.

GONZALO
Did you say Caliban?

MIRANDA
Yes. Caliban.

GONZALO
Even though he is nothing much to look at?
Then he is a fortunate man, indeed.

MIRANDA

We maligned and mistreated him for years,
And I am accessory to this crime.
Fortune, in a sudden flash of light, opened
My eyes to his true worth and revealed
His soul to me. And remembering
My father's precept to look well beyond
What the eyes can see, beyond the visible,
I now know where my affections lie.

GONZALO

Good philosophy, and I second it,
For often we are misled by glossy masks,
And such nonsense that take our eyes and sense.
Then you have given up on Ferdinand?

MIRANDA

I have, good Gonzalo. He is handsome,
Even though my father had said that
To the most of men he is a Caliban,
And others are angels to him. But beauty
Is second to character, and Ferdinand
Has no character to speak of.

GONZALO

Your father's a learned man, but not wise,
Having immersed himself in esoteric
And forbidden lore. His judgement sometimes
Begs to be questioned. Beauty is in the eye
Of the beholder, and if you can see beauty
In Caliban, then you deserve all the credit
I can give.

MIRANDA

What am I to do? I love him.
I've got used to seeing him around,
Feeling kinship with him. It's as though
We have been married all these years here.

GONZALO

Your sudden falling in love with Fernando
Was not natural for it was brought about
By your father's artful machinations.

MIRANDA

Most unnaturally, it was effected
Through his magic, and is null and void.

GONZALO

This island, Miranda, is Paradise,
And you and Caliban are Adam and Eve.

MIRANDA

What a strange idea!
Not once my father spoke of Adam and Eve,
A story he so loved to dwell upon.
But why do you call Caliban Adam?

GONZALO

I've heard your father call Caliban earth,
And earth is Adam in a language you don't know.

MIRANDA

What is it?

GONZALO

An ancient language in which sacred texts
Were written -- Hebrew, a language spoken
By God in Creation. By calling him earth,
Your father acknowledged his humanity.

MIRANDA

I knew all along that he had a heart,
And feelings, no less than any of us.

GONZALO

You grew up on this heavenly island.
Here you'll lack nothing for most of the land
Is fertile, with apples and berries and fresh springs.
Stay here, marry this man, be fruitful and multiply.

MIRANDA

You say so?

GONZALO

    Yes, and I repeat it. Stay.
Caliban is nature and has his own sweet
Innocence, while you are a nymph of the sea.
And hear this: I too will stay here, for it suits
My vision of unadulterated perfection.
Here we shun filial plots, of brother
Against brother, ambition, greed, bribery,
Torture, murder, and a hundred forms
Of unnatural criminalities.

MIRANDA

You are putting me in poetic mood,
And I'm wrapped up in a lethargic dream.

GONZALO

We are such stuff that dreams are made of,
For our little life is but a cobweb
Of concepts, visions, images, moods
And illusions, surfing the cross currents
Of our imagination, and this island
Is soothing paradise to dream away
This slipping and slippery life of ours.

MIRANDA

What shall my father say to such a venture?
Will he not say I am out of my mind?

GONZALO

Let him say whatever, and I'll be branded
A lunatic too. Your father, Miranda,
Has delved too much into books, gone astray,
Read too much and landed on magic,
And there is no clear line between white
And black magic. And I now remember one
Doctor Faustus, a brilliant man who
Was tempted to sell his soul to the devil
In exchange for immortality, which no man
Can possibly attain.

MIRANDA

Oh, heaven forbid that my father should
Do such an ungodly thing! I shudder to think
Of it.

Enter Prospero.

PROSPERO

What is that you said about your father?
What have you been teaching her, Gonzalo?

GONZALO

Teaching nothing but good precepts, Prospero.
I dare not meddle in family affairs.

MIRANDA

Father, I will stay here on this island.
I grew up here among its trees, shrubs,
And springs. I'm a fairy of this blessed land.

PROSPERO

Enough senseless blabber, or I'll begin
To hate thy sight and shun thee like a plague.
What will you do here, foolish wench? What?
Catch fish, trap a butterfly, chase a monkey?

MIRANDA

All these, and more. I will marry Caliban.

PROSPERO

Marry, what? Who?

MIRANDA

Caliban. He proposed to me.

PROSPERO

Oh, heavens! Repeat what you've just said, fool.
Marry what? That devil who plotted my death?
Oh, what an idiot to bring forth lizards
In human shape, an ungrateful breed.
You wish to marry Caliban, that misshapen

Ugly thing? Remember, you called him villain,
And many a time you loathed the sight of him.

MIRANDA
It was you and your constant tirade that
Made me biased against him. He is not
The monster you've made of him; it's you
Who have turned him into this thing you hate.
I may be your daughter but I am not
A thing to be controlled any more.

PROSPERO
I can hardly believe my ears, or else I'm mad.
Good Gonzalo, speak to her, make her see
Some sense. I am lost, lost, I tell you.
All I've seen here is betrayal. Betrayal
By my own brother, betrayal by Alonso,
And now betrayal by my spirit, Ariel,
Who has absconded with my magic tools
And handed them to villainous Caliban.
And here my daughter seeks to desert me
And marry my slave and potential killer.
I'll soon have to call this monkey my son.

GONZALO
Sir, be not offended by what I have to say.
You know how much I've loved and honoured you,
How much loyalty I had to your dukedom,
How much I abhorred your enemies' plots --
That of your brother, Antonio, and his
Collaborator, Alonso, king of Naples;
How much I detested their ambition and greed,
But your daughter is right …

PROSPERO
Right? Have you gone mad, Gonzalo?

GONZALO
Perhaps I too gone mad. We've all gone mad
On this enchanted island, this blessed piece
Of land in the middle of nowhere.
What else to do here but to go mad!
Yes, we are all gone mad, except your daughter
Who, at last, can see light amid this pitch darkness
You have conjured up.

PROSPERO
Accusing me? Pointing your finger at me?

GONZALO
Be not amazed to see your loyal friend
Turn against you when he sees how wrong
You are. Give him thanks for honesty, sir.
You've gone beyond the limits of legitimate
Inquiry. You've trespassed into forbidden
Fields, tabooed areas, quicksand that has a trap
Big enough to swallow anybody, whole.

PROSPERO
You, too? You whom I have always loved?

GONZALO
Let me be quite blunt with you, Prospero,
Since we are here on no man's land, all equal.
You are unfit to govern, sir. You are
A dreamer, an intellectual fraud,
Not a politician who can manage people.
Your true strength lies in airy nothings,

In using marionettes populated
By spirits and images, wherein you show
Your bookish strength. In a dukedom
Populated by men, you are a failure,
Sorely unfit to govern.

PROSPERO
Keep heaping abuse on me, Gonzalo.
I deserve every word coming from you,
You who saved my life, providing me with
Physical and spiritual sustenance when
Those devils dumped my daughter and me
Into a bark and left us to the hazards
Of the sea and its turbulent waves.

Enter Caliban.

How now, you miscreant, you rapist,
You who sought to violate the honour
Of my chaste daughter, monstrous thing!
And will you now wish to steal my jewel
From me, thief?

CALIBAN
Calling me names will not help you a thing.
About what you call potential rape,
You are, as usual, way far mistaken.
It's your sick imagination at work.
Your daughter happened to trip and fall
And I helped her to her feet, whereupon
She panicked, claimed assault, and cried rape.
It's you who had planted the seeds of this
Monstrous lie, this bias. She had always

Heard you speak ill of me. You've frozen
Her thoughts and feelings to suit your own.

PROSPERO
Miranda, didn't he try to rape you?

MIRANDA
I don't know. I cannot tell. But he's right
To say you have always berated him.

CALIBAN
I could not have laid a finger on this
Precious nymph of this island of mine.
Your lies seek to justify your claim to this land,
To your violation of my natural rights,
Your appropriation of my inheritance.
And don't go around telling people you were
Kind enough to let me lodge in your cell,
With you and your daughter close by.
It's just another lie you've spread about
To cover up your designs, for since when
Natives were allowed such hospitality?
Since when a monkey said to smell like fish
Was allowed to share the same roof with royalty?

GONZALO
I now recall a most bizarre story
Of an English virgin visiting India
Who, having entered a Marabar cave,
Gone hallucinating, and blamed her
Innocent Indian host for sexual misconduct.

MIRANDA

It's his brainwashing me, day in day out,
About the sexual promiscuity of natives.
That girl must have had a secret urge for
A male encounter, and the poor man was
Her target -- an easy prey, being native.

CALIBAN

Yes, natives. We are reputed to having
Our private parts ever ready to salaam
And perform at will.

PROSPERO

Go now and trap some fish for our guests;
And get us wood for cooking. Get thee hence,
And for thy insults, tonight there will be
Pinches and bites by my loyal ministers.

CALIBAN

You are now in my power, Prospero.
The chores you mentioned are yours to perform.
Take note!

> *Exeunt* all.

****

Scene 3

A place near Prospero's cell.

> *Enter* Fernando and Miranda.

MIRANDA
Do not pursue me. I am resolute
In my decision.

FERNANDO
But what do you see in him?

MIRANDA
I see in him what I don't see in you.
We grew up together on this island,
And though apart, I used to watch him,
His body and soul aching, getting abuse
From father who taught me to shun
And revile him. But he is no monster.
We are the monsters.

FERNANDO
What?

MIRANDA
I said we are the monsters.

FERNANDO
So young and so crooked!

MIRANDA
So young and such a bigot!
Can't you see, we are already fighting.
We are not fit for each other. What fits
Are our titles, which don't count towards
A happy marriage.

FERNANDO
Giving up on a kingdom, pretending

Your cave is a king's palace?

MIRANDA
I have no wish to live in a king's palace --
A prison rife with intrigue, not knowing
When my throat would be slit, or my head
Be chopped off for some trumped up rumour.
If my happiness lodges in a cave,
Then let me dwell in a cave.

FERNANDO
Chicken!

MIRANDA
I may be chicken, but I'm not for cooking.

FERDINAND
Yet fit for roasting. You're throwing away
A kingdom with its civilization,
Clinging to this wild island of yours,
Where your cave of happiness may cave in.
You're day-dreaming.

MIRANDA
     What do you know of dreams?
You've lived a life of sordid reality,
Surrounded by pomp and circumstance
That left you with scant imagination.

FERNANDO
Oh what a rude girl you are! Queen of Insults.

          Exeunt separately.

ACT THREE

Scene 1

Before Prospero's cell.

> *Enter* Prospero and Alonso, *and then* Sebastian, Antonio, and Gonzalo.

PROSPERO
I trust you all had a good night sleep.

ALONSO
Never had I such sweet sleep, such repose.
Some soft music charmed my ears and soul
As though coming from a distant planet,
And led me to sleep.

PROSPERO
    It is not magic, sir.
This island has been home to sundry spirits,
Who when the right mood prompts them, play
On our fancy most enchantingly,
With music that flows in harmony with
The tenor of their feelings.

GONZALO
I wish I could say the same. My sleep
Was uneven.

ALONSO
    And what could have been the reason?

GONZALO
Intruding thoughts, questionings that pester.
Your Highness, I joined you on this journey
As your councillor.

ALONSO
    We hold you in high esteem.

PROSPERO
Gonzalo has something weighty on his mind.

ALONSO
Open your heart and unload your mind.
We shall take any rebuke you wish
To administer, as any medicine
That a physician would prescribe,
Be it so ever bitter.

ANTONIO [Aside to Sebastian.]
We should have poisoned him.

SEBASTIAN [Aside to Antonio.]
Timing was the thing.

ALONSO
Do not hesitate, honest Gonzalo.

GONZALO

Prospero here has rashly pardoned persons
Who committed unpardonable crimes.

PROSPERO

You are talking of my brother Antonio,
And His Highness' brother, Sebastian.

GONZALO

Yes.

ALONSO

Some brothers!

GONZALO

Heads are chopped off in England for crimes
Much less drastic. Repentance and forgiveness
Have their proper place but are poor substitutes
For good administration of government.
Let them first feel the weight of just punishment,
Or else, state crimes would become commonplace.

ALONSO

We thank you for this admonition, sir.
What think you, Prospero?

PROSPERO

I admit I've forgiven half heartedly.
I can only speak of Antonio, though.
I grant it's not enough for him to hand me back
My dukedom. Some appropriate penalty
Should be exacted.

GONZALO
>   And be aware,
As only Prospero fully knows,
Both Antonio, and Sebastian the king's brother,
Conspired to kill both the king and me.

ALONSO
Most incredible! Is this true, Sebastian?

PROSPERO
He cannot deny it for Ariel and I
Have recorded it as irrefutable fact.

SEBASTIAN
I must acknowledge it, to my shame.

ALONSO
Your shame? Is that all you have to say?
How could you think of such a heinous crime --
To kill your brother who's also your king?

PROSPERO
A most unnatural scheme to contemplate;
To reenact the primeval crime.

ALONSO
How can good wombs bear such unnatural brothers!
I am utterly speechless.

GONZALO
Sir, it has nothing to do with wombs.
It has to do with greed and ambition,
Twin thieves that need vigilance at all times.

ALONSO
Prospero?

PROSPERO
Let me first ask Antonio his reasons
For usurping my rightful dukedom.

ANTONIO
Sir, seeing your library was more precious
To you than your dukedom -- as you once bragged --
It became clear to me and to others,
That you were unfit to govern Milan.
You are far better a philosopher
Than a politician; a gifted pilot
Of ideas than of dukedoms. In a word,
As our honest councillor here has said:
As ruler, you proved yourself a failure.
You claim your citizens loved you. Perhaps.
But they laughed at you behind your back
On account of your stark incompetence.
Deny what I've just said, if you can.

PROSPERO
There's some truth in what you say, I admit.
But you are still a usurper to which crime
You dumped me and my daughter in a boat,
Both exposed to the perils of the sea --
Not much different from a death sentence.

ANTONIO
With you at the helm, Milan was bereft
Of a navigator and was doomed to sink.
Such a disaster would've been a worse crime.
Your dukedom is now back in your hands,

And I will accept a judge's verdict
Regarding my own wrongdoings.

PROSPERO
Gonzalo, how would you act on this issue.

GONZALO
I would disarm both him and Sebastian,
Lest they change their mind and entertain
Further mischief.

PROSPERO
Would your Highness agree to this?

ALONSO
A most sagacious advice, Gonzalo.
Once back in our cities, we will submit
These so-called brothers to a judge's verdict.

GONZALO
With mitigating circumstances, and so
Short of a hanging or a life sentence.
Then true repentance and heart-felt forgiveness
Would be most fitting.

ALONSO [To Sebastian and Antonio.]
You have heard what Gonzalo has just said.

> *Sebastian and Antonio take off their swords and throw*
> *them aside.*
>
> [*Arguing voices in the background.*]
>
> *Enter* Fernando and Miranda.

[Miranda holding a bouquet of flowers behind her back.]

MIRANDA

No wonder you played me false at chess.
You are not the man I wish to wed.
Stop chasing after me.

FERNANDO

How can you renege on your solemn word
Of marriage? Fickle, I say, fickle.

MIRANDA

The wonder has vanished, sir. I take back
My marriage proposal.

ALONSO

What's the matter, Fernando?
Have you somewhat offended her?

FERNANDO

No, I did not. Her words of affection
Suddenly turned sour, and she's annulling her
Marriage vow.

MIRANDA

I never vowed to marry you.

ALONSO

Alas! What do you make of this, Prospero?

PROSPERO

I can make nothing of it, sir.

MIRANDA
It was an arranged marriage, anyhow.

ALONSO
What do you mean by arranged marriage?
Who arranged it?

MIRANDA
That man standing next to you -- my father.
My love for Ferdinand, if love it was,
Was staged by him. He had his Ariel spirit
Make us fall in love, as it were.

PROSPERO
I am afraid it is true.

ALONSO
How could you tamper with what should be
A matter of the heart, not to be mediated
By any supernatural agency?

MIRANDA
My father sought to make me Queen of Naples.
He has perfected his art of raising storms
Wrecking ships, and sealing marriages.

ALONSO
Ha! So, that's the reason for this romance,
This make-believe love-at-first-sight?

PROSPERO
I admit that much.

ALONSO

Matchmaker, eh?
Our honest councillor here is quite right
About ambition and greed. It seems
All of us, in power, are guilty of it.
And, Miranda, why is it you reject
Your father's shrewd scheme to make you queen?

MIRANDA

I am not a plaything, sir. My marriage
Is my own concern, my true happiness,
Or my despair. I am not to be arranged
And rearranged. It is not a game at chess.

ALONSO

A game at chess!
Aptly answered and, for that answer,
I wish you would reconsider. I would
Love to call you daughter.

MIRANDA

It would be an honour to call you father,
Your Highness, but alas, it cannot happen.

FERNANDO

With his tricks and hidden agenda, he
Also heaped abuse on me, saying,
To most men I am a Caliban and they
To me are angels. I was also made
To do heavy lifting of wood, as though
I was a slave. He claimed he had to prove
My love for this arrogant girl, whose nose
Is high up in the air.

ALONSO
Did you insult my one and only son?

PROSPERO
It was much more of a test than insult.
I did it to cool my daughter's fervour
And your son's impetuousness, sir.
She had seen no youth before seeing him.

ALONSO
Then it has been quite a short engagement.
My son was just a novelty for her.

MIRANDA
Yes, he was just a novelty for an hour.
I am now engaged to someone else.

ALONSO
Someone else?
Who could be better than my son?

MIRANDA
Caliban.

ALONSO
Who?

MIRANDA
Caliban.

ALONSO
Caliban?

SEBASTIAN
Caliban?

ANTONIO
Caliban?

MIRANDA
Yes, Caliban. Have you all gone deaf?
We grew up together on this island.
While father was poring over his books,
Or practising his black or white magic,
Caliban and I played hide and seek,
Or chased butterflies, or plucked chicken,
Or set the table for breakfast or dinner.
We laughed and frolicked as little children,
Then one day my father wrongly accused him
Of a crime my heart shudders to name --
That of attempted rape, which was not true.
My father always mistreated him, yet
I felt pity for him seeing him wronged;
Pity, which I hid beneath a heap of rubble,
For I always knew he was innocent.
And if he seems unattractive to you
It is because you do not really know him.
And I concede he is not much to look at,
But I have seen others not much to think of.
And now I know he has a place in my heart.
And, having seen a sample of the brave
New world, I must say I have lost all wish
To see more of it, let alone to wed it.

ALONSO
This piece of news would certainly cure deafness.
What have you to say about this, Prospero?

PROSPERO
Much of it is already known to me.
I'm now powerless; called a lame duck.
I have lost my tools of magic and you've
Just now advised me not to tamper with
Matters of the heart. But where is Caliban?

GONZALO
There he is!

> *Enter* Caliban, dressed in Prospero's robe [now trimmed to fit] but without his book and staff.

CALIBAN
Caliban is here!

> [Miranda, holding the bunch of flowers, runs to join him, with a hug.]

I've taken time to get rid of this man's
Diabolic tools -- his magic book and staff.
The one I threw into the sea, the other
I destroyed, making it inoperable.
Prospero here has wronged me, having usurped
My kingdom, under false pretexts,
These twelve long years. As usurper, he has
Heaped physical and mental abuse on me.
He used the airy spirits of this paradise
To torture me with cramps, hounds and goblins.
He preached many a sermon on grace

But proved himself ungraceful and ungodly.
An apology addressed to me is mere wind,
Yet it is imperative and I demand it,
In the presence of these witnesses.

PROSPERO
My deeds upon my head! I sought to improve
My mind, but ended perverting it sorely.
My magic, this thing of darkness, I
Acknowledge was mine, and I hereby
Abjure and renounce it for ever.
What can I say to justify my cruelties?
I did trespass on this island of yours,
To which I have neither natural nor legal right.
Reparations, rest assured, I'm willing to make.

CALIBAN
I accept your apology. I forgive.
But, mark you well, I will not forget.
As to reparations, your daughter is
The prize you have unwittingly paid.

ALONSO
Councillor, what's your take on this matter?

GONZALO
He is the owner of this island.

CALIBAN
    King!

GONZALO
Yes, king. And it would be fitting to crown
Him king, and you, Alonso, being king,

Would become your office to crown him one.

ALONSO
With all my heart, provided we all get
Safe passage to our ship -- which Prospero
Has told me, is safe and sound -- and depart
In peace after the ceremony.

CALIBAN
No fear! You are all under my protection.
I'll show this bigot here the difference
Between my native culture and his own.

ALONSO
What shall we use for crown?

MIRANDA
These fresh flowers will make a proper one.

ALONSO
Antonio and Sebastian will do just that;
A duty that'll count towards their punishment.

[Antonio and Sebastian proceed to making a crown.]

Enter Adrian and Francisco, followed by Stephano
and Trinculo.

FRANCISCO
While we were nearby exploring the island,
We found these two drunk bums lounging about,
Talking obscenities loudly.

ALONSO
Back in Naples they will get their deserts.

TRINCULO
Stephano is now king of this island!

STEPHANO
My word is law here.

ALONSO
My butler is washed over with alcohol.

PROSPERO
He floated to shore on a butt of a wine sack.

TRINCULO
He is now King, and I am his butler.

Enter the Master, Boatswain, and two Mariners.

ALONSO
Here's more of us. Welcome, welcome!

BOATSWAIN
I don't believe in miracles, but this is one.
We followed drunken voices, and here we are
Led by excess wine to you. Our ship is safe
And ready to take you back to Naples.

GONZALO
As I prophesied, this man was not for drowning
But for dry death.

ALONSO
He shall yet live and lead us back to Naples.
But before we embark on our journey,
There's crowning to be done and a kingdom
To set up.

MASTER
   Is all this real or not?

GONZALO
It's all real, sir. Use your hands to see
How real everything is.

   [Sebastian hands the finished crown to Alonso who
   proceeds to place it on Caliban's head.]

ALONSO
In my authority as King of Naples,
I crown you king and owner of this island.

ALL
Hail, King Caliban! Hail, King Caliban!
Long live King Caliban!

   [Everyone files to congratulate him.]

STEPHANO
Won't you have me as your butler?

CALIBAN
You are welcome to be my foot-licker.

STEPHANO
Most obediently, Your Highness!

CALIBAN
You turned out to be a false god, a fool,
Claiming you dropped out from the moon.
But next time you are swept to this shore,
Bring with you some of that celestial liquor.

TRINCULO
I prithee be my god.

[Laughter is heard.]

GONZALO
Quiet please!
Miranda has an announcement to make.

MIRANDA
My fiancée and I wish to be married
Before you leave this island.

[Miranda and Caliban look tenderly at each other
and embrace.]

PROSPERO
You expect me to call that thing son?

MIRANDA
He's as human as you and I. Acknowledge!
Many a time I heard you calling him earth,
And God made Adam out of plain earth.

PROSPERO
So you are now Adam and Eve, eh?

MIRANDA
Yes. And this is our Garden of Eden.

GONZALO
Prospero, we have a wedding on our hands.
Let us celebrate. Any more provisions
Left in your cell?

PROSPERO
    Plenty and to spare.
Salted fish, venison, berries and walnuts,
And much more. I'll get all I can lay my hands on.

ALONSO
Lords, won't you give him a hand? We'll all eat.

[Prospero goes to his cell, followed by Adrian and
Francisco.]

STEPHANO
I'll be damned. All of this looks quite real.

TRINCULO
As real as Swiss cheese. I am starved.

STEPHANO
And I am famished.

[Prospero and the two lords return with provisions.]

ALONSO
Won't you all help make a good round table
For all to share in this plenty.

[All sit in a circle and everyone eats with relish.]

GONZALO
Let's make this a most memorable occasion
For this lucky and happy pair.

[Some rise and sing and dance.]

MIRANDA [To Caliban.]
Do you love me?

CALIBAN
With all my heart, my one and only wonder,
My beautiful, nonpareil Miranda.

Enter Ariel [Visible to Caliban only.]

CALIBAN [To Ariel.]
What brought you here?

ARIEL
A surprise visit to a good, old friend.
But, truly, I had inkling some festivity
Was taking place.

CALIBAN
   My crowning and my wedding.

ARIEL
I congratulate you on your wedding,
King Caliban! Enjoy your marital bliss.
She will become your bed.

CALIBAN

She already has!

ARIEL

Brave mate!

[Ariel sings.]

Hail, Caliban and Miranda,
King and Queen exciting wonder!
A pair never such seen
On an island so green.
May you never know sadness nor sigh;
In joy increase and multiply.

Any mission required?
Shall I raise a storm and shipwreck those sinners?

CALIBAN

Leave them to heaven and the elements.

AREIL

Then forgive all my transgressions, I beg.

CALIBAN

Poor soul, you too have a conscience?
I forgive you everything. Go in peace.

ARIEL

Fare thee well. Call me any time you need me.

Exit Ariel.

[All rise to extend good wishes to the couple. Prospero and Caliban hug.]

CALIBAN
Do come after eight months. You will see
A litter of little Calibans around.
And make sure you don't put us on the map
As we would prefer to be left alone,
With no visitors of any kind at all.
And, mark you this: any missionary
Setting foot on this island, by chance
Or design, his fate is sealed and will be
Nourishment for this island's birds of prey.

MIRANDA
No missionaries, father. Remember that.

PROSPERO
Make sure your issue learns our language.
How else would I communicate with the little ones?

MIRANDA
Not to worry. They can be bilingual.

CALIBAN
I'll teach them how to warble.

ALONSO
Gonzalo has decided to stay here.
We wish all you three the best of wishes.

CALIBAN
He is now my dear honest councillor.

BOATSWAIN
We should think of the tide before it turns
Against us.

ALONSO
Yes, yes. We are all ready to depart.

GONZALO
This is the perfect commonwealth for me.
How fortunate I am to find it at last.
Here I'll live my last days amid green elves
And jolly spirits. Farewell, all of you.

ALL
Farewell, King and Queen. Farewell Gonzalo!
Farewell Caliban! Farewell Miranda!

> *Exeunt omnes.*

EPILOGUE

Spoken by Gonzalo and Ariel

Enter Gonzalo

We have come to end of play,
And here's what I have to say:
Prospero is a sinner like the rest;
With magic did his mind infest.
Away with greed and ambition;
Hence betrayal and sedition!
This island's now my paradise,
Won through other people's vice.
Here equality will rule,
With scant room for a fool.
This heaven is sheer illusion,
Where dreams are no delusion.
Here I'll dwell amid plenty
To hundred years and twenty.
Miranda found her king and kingdom,
Caliban his freedom and health,
And I, my sweet commonwealth.

Exit Gonzalo.

Enter Ariel

My hero now is Caliban
For Prospero was a wicked man.
Catholic in his wizardry,
Was master of slavery.
Inquisitive to third degree,
Excelled in cruelty.
Let no missionary come hither,
And may all colonials wither!
There's nothing like liberty,
Care's gone when one's free.
My slave-master is now gone,
And I feel like newly-born.
Shackled slaves in adversity,
Caliban and I, now mates in liberty.
Let's hear your big applause --
High and mighty -- without a pause.

Exit Ariel.

The End

14262748R00058